THE JESUS
I FORGOT

*Have We Sacrificed Obedience
on the Altar of Reason?*

Lane Payne

ISBN 979-8-89243-710-3 (paperback)
ISBN 979-8-89243-711-0 (digital)

Christian Faith Publishing
832 Park Avenue
Meadville, PA 16335
www.christianfaithpublishing.com

Printed in the United States of America

Contents

Introduction

There are myriads of books written concerning the person of Jesus. Some are written to reveal a particular thought about His character, and others speak of detailed discoveries concerning His history. This book is a memoir of my own personal experiences centered around the power of the name of Jesus.

I am inviting you to join me as we travel through my journey. While this recounting of my personal expedition is very personal to me, I am convinced that along the way, you will discover some of your own struggles.

It is my greatest desire that something is going to grab hold of your heart and lead you to one of two conditions of the heart: (1) either you will find your way back to the lordship of Jesus, or (2) you will find that Jesus is a loving and trustworthy Lord for the first time in your life.

As you trek alongside this time line of highs and lows, you are going to be exposed to some things, which may be difficult for some to read. But by continuing through to the end, I am convinced that you just might see Jesus from a totally different perspective.

Let's go…

Chapter 1

Hardships Growing Up

My youngest memories of growing up centered around some very difficult times as my mom (Kaye) and dad (Tommy) fought often, at least verbally. With every heated episode came another trip with my mom taking me in that old Chevy El Camino to the Tiger Drive Inn on Airline Highway in Baton Rouge. I am convinced we saw every single one of Elvis Presley's movies during that time (1960s).

While my dad majored on the very harsh side, it was not a cakewalk with my mom either. I remember once when she was pregnant for my little brother, Jimbo, she left me (age seven) home to go to the store, even though the doctor had specifically forbidden her to drive.

I was raised in a home which demanded absolute obedience or pay the harsh consequences. As I watched her drive off, driven by fear for her, I went to my neighbor's house to tell a friend about how she was disobeying the doctor. But when she was driving into the driveway, she saw me running back to our house.

I remember how frightened I was as she tore into me with a belt but also knew that the entire ordeal was not over

1

because I still had to face my dad. When he came home later, I could hear her angrily telling him what I had done and how he needed to whip my behind again.

When he came into the room and saw the results of what she had already done to me, he asked her, "What do you want me to do, finish him off?" So he didn't add anything to the punishment I had already taken.

The reality is that my mom's pregnancy wasn't supposed to happen because the doctor had told her she should not have any children after I was born due to her physical complications, but she was a South Louisiana Cajun woman who wasn't about to let a doctor tell her how many children she could have.

Mom had major complications in the delivery of my baby brother that led to multiple surgeries concerning those complications: a colostomy and two other surgeries within six months. She contracted hepatitis from the resulting blood transfusions and died when Jimbo was nearly seven months old.

One year later, my dad remarried to my present mom, Dianne, who already had three boys; Teddy, Tommy, and David; and a daughter, my sister, Anita. I was fast becoming more and more bitter toward this entire situation, especially when my dad, wanting to show my new brothers what would happen to them if they disobeyed him, gave me a belt whipping for absolutely no other reason than to give them an example of what it meant to cross him.

At that point, I went from being a little bitter to actually hating. Anytime my new brothers and I got into an argument, I would literally try to hurt them just to take out my frustrations on them. I thank God I was a skinny little thing and therefore could not inflict too much harm.

My dad had a unique way of handling all the arguments that came up between me and my brothers. Anytime we had an argument, he would make us put on boxing gloves and tell us to start fighting. He would beat whoever was losing on their back with a belt until they were winning, then he would beat the other one because they were losing. I had one mindset during those times: Don't take it personal if I try to rip your head off. I just have to keep this belt off of my back!

Needless to say, I grew up with an *engrained respect* for my dad's authority. Whenever he wanted to drill home a demand, he would say it like this: "If you don't think that I'll stomp a mud hole in you, just try me hand." He usually called us all *hand* because there ended up being six boys and a girl by the time my baby brother Blake came along, and he would get our names confused.

Dad was really hard on us, especially when it came to school. I remember him telling me that he quit school in the ninth grade just because he could. That one pivotal point in his life became his entire motivation toward us and our education, at least in his mind. He felt that if his dad had forced him to finish school, he would have finished.

In his heart, he was determined to not make the same mistake with us, so he used the only known weapon in his arsenal: *anger.*

> How often does the pendulum swing too far in the opposite direction when we are trying to figure out how to do a better job of bringing up our children than the way we were brought up?

My dad was brought up in a generation that still had the lingering effects of Christian values from a nation birthed on the word of God, even though they were not a churchgoing family. I remember him not growing a garden one year. And when I asked him why, he said, "You have to let the ground recover in the seventh year. That is what the Bible says."

As I pondered this reality later on in life, I came to realize that God's standards live on through generations. But when it eventually fades in one generation, it becomes completely void in the next. This is why our nation seems to be void of Christian values today.

There were only two standards I recalled growing up: hard work and absolute respect for authority! My dad could not stand the opposite of either, and he had no problem revealing the depths of his feelings concerning both.

I remember growing up and seeing other kids talking back to their parents and thought, *I would rather try to take a steak from a hungry lion than try that with my dad!*

Because we were brought up in a non-Christ-centered home, there were myriads of issues that we dealt with during those years, too many and too harsh to recount. As I look back at my childhood, I can remember the hunting trips, the times fishing, and a few campouts. But there is one thing that I cannot ever remember: being held, consoled, or encouraged not even once.

My wife of over forty-three years now and the love of my life on this side of heaven asked me why I never wanted to have anything to do with horses. I had never thought about it until she asked. But when she did, the memories came flashing back.

I was about ten years of age when my dad and I went horseback riding at a bird dog field trial with some of his friends. We rode horses for a good portion of the day.

That evening, about bedtime, I was unusually sore from the day's events, and I made the critical mistake of complaining about it to my dad, and he came in the room and started beating me with a belt, to the point that my mom had to come into the room, trying to stop him. I guess that might have had something to do with my distaste for horseback riding.

Though I am revealing some of the harsh circumstances of my early years, I have to say that it is not to bring dishonor to my dad. I am so thankful to God for bringing me up under Tommy Payne. I believe that God was forging something deep inside of me that I never saw coming and would not have planned out for myself in my natural mind. I am not saying that God caused these things to happen, but God saw them and had a plan to use them for His own glory.

> If you are thinking, *How could a loving God allow such hardship?* well, here you go… I grew up with a complete fear of my dad. But when I got saved, it turned into a complete fear of the Lord. The fear of my dad was unhealthy, but when God saved me, He turned everything around. I will cover that detail later on…

And we know that all things work together for good to those who love God, to those who are the called according to His purpose. (Romans 8:28 NKJV)

When I became a senior at Baker High School in Baker Louisiana, I was invited to go to a church service at Bethany World Prayer Center. I had never been to any other church besides a Catholic Church or the Baker Presbyterian Church, so I thought it would be a similar experience. Boy, was I in for a shock. I had even responded to the alter, and it felt amazing. But just as quickly as those feelings came is just how fast they faded.

> When anyone hears the word of the kingdom, and does not understand it, then the wicked one comes and snatches away what was sown in his heart. This is he who received seed by the wayside. (Matthew 13:19 NKJV)

Isn't it amazing, when we initially experience the presence of God, how quickly and without our recognition the devil diverts our attention to the things of this world?

As soon as I graduated high school, I moved in with my grandmother on my birth mom's side in Abbeville, Louisiana. My thought process was to get away from the pain and find my own way.

Little did I know that God had something far greater in mind. That is where I met the woman I was born to spend the rest of my life with, Brenda Connor.

Chapter 2

Married at Nineteen

I had just left Baker in 1979 and moved in with my grandmother in Abbeville, Louisiana, when I met this beautiful Cajun girl at a very small store. It was actually part house and part tiny neighborhood store. Brenda was working at that tiny neighborhood store, and I made it my business to go by there whenever I could just to see her.

I had a temporary summer job, working as a bricklayer's laborer while staying at my grandmother's house in preparation for going to college. I would tell my grandparents all about this girl named Brenda when I would come home from work because I would go by the store on the way home. But what I didn't know was that my grandfather was going back to the store and telling Brenda everything I was telling him about her. He was our own personal cupid.

After work one day, I went to check on my uncle's car wash because he and his family were on vacation. I was about one-half mile from the car wash when I started struggling to stay awake. I had been having trouble sleeping due to working in the extreme South Louisiana August heat, and that is when it happened: I fell asleep at the wheel of a 1970 Camaro, going about 70 mph.

The car hit the railing on a bridge, flipped upside down in the air, flew over a canal, which was about twenty-five feet wide, and landed upside down in the roadside ditch.

The hood of the car folded in half, came through the windshield, bent the steering wheel down, and pinned against the driver's seat. I should have been decapitated, but I was somehow pushed down between the seats, and the hood came right over my left side. The glass from the windshield sliced through my face and neck, gashing holes on the way through.

I had holes in my face and a silver-dollar-size hole in my neck, exposing my jugular vein. The doctor said, "Another 1/32 of an inch deeper, and you would not have gotten out of the car!" I took seventeen stitches in my face and neck, along with cuts on my hands and arms.

The very next day, with massive headaches due to the resulting concussion and with my face, neck, and arms all bandaged, my grandmother sent me to that little store, which was only two blocks away, to get some groceries. *WOW, really!* I didn't say it, but I was definitely thinking it.

So with my hair matted up and stitches in my face and neck, off I went to the store, both confused and a little frustrated, not even thinking about how I would look to Brenda.

What I did not know was that my grandfather had already told her the entire story. When I walked into the store, she looked at me and laughingly said, "You didn't croak on me, did ya?" We both laughed, and it was ten months later that we were married on my nineteenth birthday.

One year later, I started working in the Lafayette Electrical Union, and as an apprentice, I was working with a journeyman electrician, who was very good at his craft and very obnoxious in the way he dealt with people. So many of the other electrical apprentices didn't want to work for him because he was so verbally abusive. It didn't bother me because the verbal abuse coming from him did not come with getting my butt whipped on top of it. This guy was a piece of cake compared to my dad.

The real difference with him was that he was always telling me about his wife's church and what was being spoken by their pastor. You must understand that the old journeyman was seemingly cursing every other word when he was telling me these stories, but there was something in his stories that intrigued me.

He spoke about the miracles that had taken place through this local pastor, and what it all came down to was all of it happened because of the power that existed in the name of Jesus.

On that same jobsite, there were some brothers hanging Sheetrock who were Christians. They were constantly talking about the name of Jesus and how the power of His name brings stability into every aspect of a person's life. One day, while I was working in an adjacent room, I could clearly hear them discussing the difference Jesus had made in their marriages. Then I heard them mention a Christian radio station called KAJN, and I immediately started listening.

As an apprentice, I had to go to an electrical apprenticeship school two nights a week for four years, and I remember listening to R. W. Schambach and Jesse Duplantis going to and from school weekly. I heard them speak about the power that comes in the name of Jesus for four straight years, and something happened inside of me about the second year: I began to believe in the power of the name of Jesus!

I started talking to Brenda about it, telling her all the stories that I was hearing. But her response quite honestly shocked me, and I quote, "I would rather see you running around in the bars than talking to me like that." This did not deter what was stirring in my heart one bit.

It was during this time that something significant started taking place: miracles!

Chapter 3

The Power of the Name of Jesus

Miracles

During this time, I found myself thinking about the *power* that comes in the name of Jesus. I must emphasize something right here, *I was not saved at this time* but began to have an absolute trust in the power of the name of Jesus. I was hearing about it in the workplace, listening to it on the radio, and constantly thinking about it within my own heart.

> The steps of a good man are ordered by the Lord, And He delights in his way. Though he fall, he shall not be utterly cast down; For the Lord upholds him with His hand. (Psalm 37:23–24 NKJV)

The Lord is amazing in all His ways. I then began to listen to the testimonies of those who walked in faith and was constantly pondering on the potential opportunities to make a stand on the name of Jesus. The more I did, the more I was anticipating actually standing on His name.

The instances of what you are about to read started taking place about eight years *before* I received Jesus as my Savior and my Lord.

On my way to work one morning, I was driving on the right-hand side of a four-lane road through Lafayette. There was a car to my left just ahead of me and going the same speed and direction. I was probably in their blind spot. A vehicle just in front of them had their blinker to turn left but had come to a stop due to oncoming traffic. When the car in front of me saw the stopped car, they jerked their vehicle into my lane before they looked, almost hitting me. Then they saw me and jerked back, slamming into the stopped car. Their vehicle hit the back right corner of the car in front of them, which caused their back end to spin into my lane.

I jerked the wheel to the right, going off the road to miss them, and there was a telephone pole right in front of me. I *screamed* the name of Jesus, closed my eyes, and yanked the steering wheel back to the left, bracing for the collision but ended up in the middle of the road with no damage.

I immediately jumped out of the vehicle and ran over to the telephone pole and looked at my tire marks, which were about half inch away from the pole. The confusing thing was that the front tires of that old Nissan pickup truck were at least three inches inside the fender well. I was in shock! I didn't know if God had pulled that pole out of the ground and let me pass under it *or* if He just let me pass through the pole.

But there was one thing I did know, standing on the name of Jesus rescued me that day.

After work that evening, I drove Brenda back to Lafayette to show her the tire marks on the ground, and she was completely astonished by what she was seeing and hearing.

While at this same jobsite, an acquaintance of my wife was having a baby, and she was at the very hospital in which I was presently working construction. There were dire compli-

THE JESUS I FORGOT

cations in the delivery of the baby, and the child was on life support. A couple of days after the birth of the child, I felt a strong urge to go and pray for the baby.

I took my lunch break and made my way to the PICU and asked the nurse if it were possible for me to pray for the baby. She told me that the doctors were talking to the family about the potential necessity of taking the child off life support. She pointed to the baby and said that the child had not breathed on her own since she was born.

I told her, "That child *will live, in Jesus's name!*" She told me I had to leave, and without even looking in that direction, I pointed at the child and said, "You need to look!"

We both looked at the same time, and the baby was kicking around. The nurse was in shock and made her way quickly to the child. Years later, I had heard word that the child graduated from kindergarten.

A few years after that event, Brenda's mom, Jeanelle, had fallen terribly sick, and the doctors were saying that she was dying. This was overwhelming to my wife, as it would be to any loving daughter.

I have to take a pause and say that my wife, Brenda, is the most dedicated family person I know. She loved her dad and mom deeply. I knew that I was second in her life because her dad was first. Her love for her dad was one of the attributes of her character that opened my heart to hers in the first place.

One night, after we were already in bed and I was completely asleep, I woke up with Brenda completely out of control, screaming and shaking my head around.

Confused by the chaos of the moment and not getting any response when asking her what was going on, I heard a voice speak to me, "Stand on My name or get off!" Immediately, I stood up, wrapped my arms around my wife, and demanded, "I command you to *loose* my wife, in Jesus's name!"

Instantly, Brenda became limp in my arms, looked at me with a near smile on her face, laid down, and went to sleep. I stayed up almost the entire night, trembling and asking God what was going on.

The next morning, I asked Brenda what had happened. She looked at me, almost perplexed, and said, "I felt something step out of me."

I had become impassioned with the power of the name of Jesus, to the point that I was witnessing to others about the power of His name. Some witnesses of the Latter-Day Saints came to our mobile home one day, and I spent more time talking to them about the name of Jesus than they spent trying to get me to read their book.

I asked them if they believed that people could still be healed in the name of Jesus because I had seen it with my own eyes. I asked them if they believed that demons could be cast out in the name of Jesus because I had seen this with my own eyes.

I had become completely convinced that there was nothing that faith in the name of Jesus could not do—nothing! Remember, I had been brought up in an environment of *absolute authority*. If Tommy Payne had authority, how much more resided in the name of Jesus?

Our oldest daughter, Brandy, at about three years old, developed what looked like sand in her urine, and it was very painful for her to relieve herself. Construction work locally had dried up, so I was out of work and staying at my dad's while looking for work in the Baton Rouge area. Brenda called me crying and asked me what we were going to do because our daughter was truly suffering. I was unemployed, broke, and had no insurance.

I told Brenda I would be there the next morning. She continued to press me for a plan, but I just continued telling her I would be there in the morning. That night, I prayed most of the night and made the two-hour drive back home the next morning. As soon as I got there, I walked up to my oldest daughter and asked, "Do you believe that God can heal you in the name of Jesus?" and she said, "If you say so, Daddy."

I laid my hands on her and prayed for God to heal her in the name of Jesus and told her to go to the bathroom.

Brenda said sternly, "Lane, what are you doing to her?" and I told Brenda, "You wait and see!" Our daughter went to the bathroom and came out and said, "Daddy, it didn't hurt at all!" I went over to the toilet and saw what seemed to be a teaspoon of sandy gravel in the bottom of the toilet, and I called Brenda over to show her.

Both Brenda and I were in tears. We were amazed, overjoyed, and confused all at the same time. Our daughter has never had that issue again, even to this day as she just turned forty.

I was desperate to find a more permanent work situation than what we were faced with at that time. I started calling my relatives back in the Baton Rouge area about the possibility of working there, even if it meant that I had to move. I was a journeyman electrician but was also the son of a plumber, so I was looking at either the construction arena or in one of the plants for work.

I was talking to Brenda about getting hired in one of the plants in the Baton Rouge area, and she asked, "What makes you think that you could get hired at a place like that?"

In that moment, I felt the boldness of God come on me, and I looked at her and said, "In Jesus's name, they are going to look at my resume and say, 'I don't know why we are hiring this kid, but let's hire him!'"

Within the next four years, I had been hired at Georgia-Pacific paper mill in Port Hudson in E/I (electrician/instrument technician) and eventually at Exxon Chemical Plant in Baton Rouge as an instrument technician.

I do not want anyone to lose focus on this reality. All of these events took place years before I gave my heart to Jesus in salvation. I know that this deals with the theology of many, but that does not take anything away from the reality of my experience.

A man with an experience is never subject to a man with an argument. (Roy Stockstill)

Chapter 4

Salvation

Transformation

Here is where the story really begins to move forward into the purpose of this book. My wife visited Bethany World Prayer Center in my hometown of Baker, Louisiana, and responded to the altar for salvation on her first visit, and it was about eight months later before I got saved, even though we were going to every Sunday morning service and eventually started attending every Wednesday night service as well.

I was so resoundingly convinced that I already knew the Lord because of my past experiences that it took eight months of sitting under the amazing teaching gift of Pastor Larry Stockstill before I realized that I was not saved. It was at a Wednesday night service, July 24, 1991, that I responded to the altar to give my life to Jesus.

I responded to the altar call that night, and when I got up off my knees, the Holy Spirit said, "It was Me who pushed you down between those seats!" *In that moment*, I knew exactly what He was saying. I should have been decapitated in that car wreck nearly twelve years prior.

For the first time in my life, I came to know what true love was!

I said these words to God in that very moment, "*You own me! I am done!*"

Instantaneously, something profound took place concerning my understanding about a relationship with authority. All I had ever known about authority, which was so sternly driven into my being was *submission*, no matter what. There was no choice in the matter; in fact, submission seemed to be more of a survival than anything resembling love. I had never known there could actually be love between those in authority and those who came under.

In that moment, I literally went from not being able to fathom what love was to being so overwhelmed by it that I was literally shaking! I *knew* right then and there that God loved me, and I surrendered to Him *completely*!

I had never been more settled and resolute about anything in my life up until that point in my life. In the altar room, the alter worker, who came in to pray with me, asked, "Do you want to receive the baptism of the Holy Ghost?" and I looked at him and said, "If you know that God has something for me, and you don't tell me, I am not going to be very happy. *I want it all, and I want it now!*" He laid hands on me, and tongues came out!

While I was waiting to meet with one of the pastors in the altar room, I remember the first prayer that I prayed after that experience: "Lord, if I live to be two hundred years old, I want as much zeal to learn about You as I have right now!"

I thank my God for being faithful to answer that prayer even through to this day.

Within a couple weeks of being saved, I remember coming across a particular set of scriptures that dug very deeply into my soul.

> Many will say to Me in that day, "Lord, Lord, have we not prophesied in Your name, cast out demons in Your name, and done many wonders in Your name?" And then I will declare to them, "*I never knew you*; depart from Me, you who practice lawlessness!" (Matthew 7:22–23 NKJV)

When I read that passage, I began to tremble because I knew that these passages were speaking directly toward my life prior to my salvation experience. I knew the power of His name, and I stood on that power all during those prior years. But I was, at the time of those miracles, in no way serving the Lord Jesus as one of His followers. The truth was, at that time, I had no idea about salvation.

The salvation aspect was so often left out of all the radio messages I listened to throughout the prior years.

Though I sat under so many tremendous messages at Bethany for those months, the entire concept of salvation was hidden from me until the Lord's ordained moment in time. My wife and I joked often that God had to save her first, because if I had received the Lord first, there would have been a fight! But in that beautiful instant, which was marked out before the foundation of the world, God saved me, and I turned the reigns of my life over to Him completely!

Or so I thought...

Coming from a background of understanding authority and accountability, the Lord began to deal with me in a deep, penetrating way.

One example: I was up early one morning praying, and I brought to the Lord a common husbandly type of prayer request: "Lord, can you change my wife in *this* area?" (All husbands can fill in what *this* is.)

Immediately, it was as if God were standing before me with His hand in a "beckoning me" gesture, and I heard Him say, "The day is coming when you will give Me an account of the woman you call your wife, and I call My daughter!"

I started shaking uncontrollably, but He wasn't done. He then said, "You will give Me an account for those two girls I loaned to you to bring up loving Me!"

I was on my face, weeping before the Lord, and eventually I stood up and responded to the Lord, "Lord, if this is how it is going to be, I don't want to live pleasing in my wife and children's eyes because they will accept whatever pleases them. I want to live pleasing in Your eyes! And even if I fall short of what You desire, it will be more than whatever they ask or think!"

I completely understood the accountability that I was going to have to give the Lord concerning my family, and that foundational moment before the Lord set a new course for my life as a husband and a dad. I had seen many children of godly families walk away from God, but I was determined that this was *not* going to happen to my daughters.

The Lord showed me that I was going to give Him an account for Him loaning me His name, *father*. I realized that the relationship I developed with my daughters would become the pattern, whereby they would relate to the Heavenly Father once they reached the age to have a relationship with Him.

How could my daughters understand their relationship with Father God if I did not train them in a way that would make this possible?

I believe there are myriads of dads out there just doing the best they can but are falling short because they are trying to do it within their own strength. I realized I could not accomplish this intense feat on my own, and it motivated me to seek His heart and His spirit and His word to lead me in the right way to lead our daughters.

My dad's fathering of me was not perfect by any stretch of the imagination, but his actions in my life are what God used to set me on a perfect course of accountability to the *only* One who is perfect.

The calling

After I was saved, about two months, while living in Baker, Louisiana, and working at Exxon Chemical Plant, I had two dreams, which came about two nights apart, and both of them had to do with Abbeville, Louisiana.

In the first dream, I was standing on Charity Street in Abbeville, witnessing about the love of Jesus to people, and this older Cajun gentleman came up to me and asked, "How are you going to tell me that Jesus loves me? My wife, she died of cancer, and my son is living with another man. How can you say that God loves me?"

In the dream, I responded to him, "Sir, not only does Jesus love you, but so do I!" and I woke up.

A couple nights later, I dreamed that I was back on Charity Street in Abbeville, pressing buttons on a security keypad, trying to get into an old building. It seemed like years had gone by, but I was still typing in security codes, trying to get in the door.

I remember the dream being so distinctly vivid that in the dream I was thinking, *What if I press a code, try to open the door, and it opens, but I accidently shut it back out of muscle memory, will I remember the code that I had just pressed?* So in the dream, I was saying the code numbers being pressed out loud, "1, 2, 4, 1… 1, 2, 4, 2… 1, 2, 4, 3…" And then, after many years of faithfully pressing the codes, the door opened.

I found myself sitting down with a group of religious leaders going over Romans, chapter 1, and making this statement, "Those who know the truth and hold it back, you do realize that you are going to answer to *God*!"

I immediately woke up. And even though it was about 2:30 a.m., I woke Brenda up and told her, "We are going back to Abbeville!" because I knew from that moment forward that God had called me to Abbeville.

Brenda responded, "Well, you can go back and visit me on the weekends!" In discussing her comment later, she revealed that she did not want to have to face who *she used to be* by going back to her hometown.

Immediately after salvation, we dove straight into the discipleship process at Bethany, and I found myself on the follow-up team after just a couple of months. One of the greatest experiences in my Christian life was the privilege of sitting at the feet of a man named Billy Hornsby every Tuesday night for about three years.

I learned how to pray for my family. I learned what it meant to be the head of my home. I learned what it meant to be a godly father to my daughters and husband to my wife. I learned what it meant to make a bold stand for the name of Jesus. Having the right person speaking straight into your life is so much more impactful than just sitting in a church service, no matter how dynamic it is. This does not take away from the necessity of faithfully attending church but reveals that just walking through the door is not enough to accomplish God's best for your life.

> "Having the right person speaking straight into your life is so much more impactful than just sitting in a church service, no matter how dynamic it is."

The Lord's handiwork was taking everything that had molded me, from my being raised in a completely authoritarian home and using it to usher me into the authority of heaven within my home, not from the position of dictator but as a Father. This is a revelation of the spiritual authority that God gives believers.

Before we were saved, my wife dealt with fear in a major way. It was to the point that if a thunderstorm came up during the night, she would get out of bed, sit in the doorway of the girl's bedroom, and smoke cigarettes until it passed. She thought that if she was close enough to the girls, she could keep anything bad from happening.

One night, as we were coming home from a church service, not long after we were saved, a thunderstorm was raging as we were about to get out of the vehicle. Brenda told the girls, "Girls, you stay in the car until Dad unlocks the door, and then you run inside!" I looked at her and said, "Girls, get out of the car with Dad!"

Brenda became furious with me and started fussing at me about all the potential disasters that could happen. I unlocked the door, found the anointing oil, went to the back of the house, and started anointing every window casing and door casing with Brenda fussing at me the entire time.

When I made it to the front door, I said, "I command every drop of fear to leave my house *now* in Jesus's name!" and immediately Brenda started chuckling and said, "Do you know how silly you looked?"

I looked at her and said, "You don't even realize what just happened! Fear just left this house and your heart!"

Brenda looked at me, stunned at what had just taken place.

I was quickly understanding that ministry was my calling, and it was completely evident.

The plant

After I gave my life to Jesus, everything changed for me. I wasn't the overtime hog at the plant that I was before, trying to work every minute I could to make as much money as possible. I was just as content to let someone else have the overtime, if it meant I could be more involved with my family and in the things of God through my church.

God began to give me so much favor at Exxon that even as I look back now, it astonishes me. I had developed a personal relationship with the person of the Holy Spirit, and I knew that He knew all things, so nothing was too difficult for Him to tackle through my life.

There were times when I was asked to get involved in complex problems, so I did what anyone would do and started asking questions about the situation. When the answer seemed out of reach in the natural, I would step aside and pray, "Okay, Holy Spirit, you know all things. Show me in Jesus's name!" Then I would step back in, follow His lead, and fix things that I had no experience or training to fix.

Sometimes they would look at me and ask, "What is it with you?" and I would tell them, "I have an unfair advantage over you, boys. I know the One who knows all things!" Of course, they did *not* want to hear anything about that, but they sure did want to take advantage of its reality when they needed.

Toward the end of my time at Exxon, there was a tremendous fire, and the reconstruction afterward was very intense and extensive. I was running two crews of construction contractors working in different areas of our unit, when my boss said, "While everything on the unit is down, they want you to head up the upgrades to the last furnace. It needs to be upgraded to the latest controls *even though we do not have any blueprints,* so you will have another crew of men."

Within a few days, he laughingly told me, "They are seeing how much they can load your wagon. You have maintenance while I go on vacation!" I literally felt like I had a basketball sitting in my stomach. I sat in my car and asked God what was going on, and He spoke clearly to me, "You can see this as something difficult, and you will still make it through because My grace is sufficient, *or* you can see this as an opportunity for Me to be glorified and breeze through this. *You choose!*"

I felt an immediate release and started facing everything ahead of me from the fresh perspective God had just given me. At the end of that massive project, the head of Exxon said that it was the most efficiently run turnaround in the history of Exxon. (It was not led by me, and I am not taking any credit for it. But through His leading, I was a part of it.)

Within months of its completion, I got the call to go on staff at Bethany World Prayer Center as an assistant pastor, and I had this thought: *Lord, You would allow a $35,000,000 event to take place at Exxon just to check my resolve? How can I not trust You!*

Fast-track into ministry

During my time at the plant, I was always active in ministry as well. I was one of the original fifty-four cell group leaders when Bethany started the cell group ministry. There were about five hundred people who would meet at what was called Gideon's Army on Saturday mornings for a prayer covering over the church, and Pastor Larry Stockstill started teaching that group about the cell group ministry.

I was saved about twenty months when I became a cell group leader, and over the next couple of years, we saw tremendous growth in the church, and most of it was through those small groups. The next couple of years, thousands had given their lives to Jesus through those small groups.

During that time, Pastor Gordon Atwell, who was the pastor immediately over me, spoke so many things into my life of which I am forever grateful. One of the things that I am most grateful for is that he imparted a heart for evangelism.

We prayed for literally thousands to give their lives to Jesus through the Two Question Test booth, which we set up annually at the Greater Baton Rouge State Fair. Watching the power of the gospel tear down religious and bitter walls instilled by the devil is one of the most gratifying experiences in life.

What a privilege to see our cell group leaders and church members embrace this event, which also stood to equip them for small group ministry.

While at Bethany, marriages were being healed, relationships were being restored, leaders were being trained, and callings were being established. I was saved three and a half years when I was asked to come *on staff* at Bethany. I didn't even know what a pastor was, then I was one.

On the day when I and several other pastors were hired on staff, one of those pastors, Hank Hennigan, asked me, "Well, Brother Lane, what do you think about all of this?" and I told him, "Training ground for Abbeville, Louisiana. That is the only reason I am here, Brother Hank!"

That group of pastors immediately entered into a two-year stint at MTI (minister's training institute) under the direct leadership of Brother Jim Clark, Pastor Larry Stockstill's father-in-law.

I just want to go on record right now and say that not only were Brenda and I saved and discipled at Bethany, but I believe that we were saved and discipled in the best of Bethany. I will never be able to express how deep my gratitude is to Pastor Larry Stockstill and all the leaders in that church, who played a part in building me and my family into who God called us to become.

All during this time, Brenda was walking right by my side. She knew that I was going to follow the Lord's lead, even if she didn't understand it.

Her comfort was in the fact that she knew I trusted God, so even if she wasn't sure about my decisions, she knew I would follow His and that He would never lead us astray!

> As the Scriptures tell us, "Anyone who trusts in him will never be disgraced." (Romans 10:11 NLT)

After being on staff for three and a half years, the Lord began revealing that it was time to move into the work He had saved and cultivated me to live in.

Chapter 5

Starting a Church

About six months before we made the move to Abbeville, Louisiana, to start the church God had put on my heart to birth, the youth pastor at Bethany, Adam McCain, came to me and said, "I hear that God is calling you to Abbeville, Louisiana. I know of an Assemblies of God Church down there, and they are looking for a youth pastor. Why don't you check it out?"

I told Adam, "Dude, I am *not* called to be a youth pastor, but I will go check into it." I set up a meeting and afterward knew that I was not called to youth ministry there. When I returned, Pastor Adam asked me how the meeting went, and I told him my feelings. He then looked at me and said, "You mark my words, the day is coming when the keys to that building are going to be put into your hands"

"I cannot pray like that!" I told him, but he responded, "I cannot help but tell you what God showed me!"

A few months later we moved to the Abbeville area, Perry, Louisiana, to be exact, just on the outside of Abbeville. We moved into our home in January of 1999 and had our first church service in our living room the following week.

We were having church services in our living room for about two years when we purchased a small building and started having services in the city. I then called for a group of pastors to come together and shared a vision of getting together once a week for prayer. That group of pastors crossed several denominational and racial lines, and we continued meeting weekly for over seventeen years.

We eventually supported the same missionaries, had joint worship services, and went on mission trips together, and for about twelve years, we drew names and swapped pulpits one Sunday a year in January.

During the fall of 2002, Abbeville was hit by Hurricane Lili. The Abbeville Assemblies of God building was the most destroyed building in the hurricane. They needed a place to meet, and we accommodated them with our little building, and they began meeting at an earlier time slot than our own service. Just a few short weeks later, their pastor resigned. That local church was in a rough place. Their pastor had resigned. Their building was destroyed, and they did not know what was coming next.

One day, after they had finished their service in our building, and we were about to start our service, one of their board members asked if they could sit through one of our services, to which we absolutely obliged. At the end of that service, he looked at me and said, "We need to talk!"

I began meeting with the board of the Abbeville Assemblies of God and eventually with their local body. The week before the Abbeville Assembly of God was to vote on me becoming their new pastor, I received an odd phone call. It was a lady from a church in Plaquemine, Louisiana area, and she explained to me that Pastor Adam McCain was coming to their church that Friday night, and he wanted to know if I could come.

It was our privilege to go and see the man who was my daughter's youth pastor while we were at Bethany. My family went and after we greeted each other with a hug, I looked at him and asked, "Do you remember what you spoke over me four years ago?"

He said, "Yes, I do."

I said, "They are voting me in as the pastor of that church this Sunday morning!"

He said, "*I told you I heard from God!*"

The vote was unanimous. We took on the project of rebuilding the existing building, which had been destroyed in the hurricane, renamed the church New Life Church of Abbeville, reset the government structure, and started with a fresh vision of *Restoring Lives to the Love of God*. This became our vision statement, and we actually put those words on the front of the church building.

Throughout the years of my Christian journey, something peculiar was happening that I did not expect. I had trusted God for everything since the day I was born again. The Lord had provided for our every need along the way. I had been working a full-time secular job as well as pastoring full time for ten straight years at this point, and not once had I seen God withhold anything we needed. But something had subtly shifted off course.

Chapter 6

The Rut

Things were no longer happening as they were before. That free-flowing of the Holy Spirit was not as evident as it had been. When this happens, we are taught to fight a little harder, to pray more diligently, to spend more time in study, and evaluate our hearts to make sure our worship is genuine.

But it almost seems as though the harder we tried, the harder it got. *Does this sound familiar to anyone?* Sure, the anointing was still there in the services, but something just didn't feel right. What was missing, what was going on? Did we need to invite someone in to speak? Did we need to get away to a conference? Did we need to call for a revival?

If you are a believer in the Lord Jesus Christ and yet frustrated in your life with Christ, I want to reveal a weapon of the devil that he has subtly spoken to you without you even hearing the words: *"It is all on you!"*

We hear so much about our prayer life making us usable to the Lord. We hear about our knowledge of the word of God making us usable to the Lord. We hear about learning to follow the leading of the Holy Spirit making us usable to the Lord. Yet while all of this *is true*, the devil is hiding in the shadows of this truth with a lie.

He is trying to get you to add your worth into the equation of God's power. I really want to help someone: There is nothing that we can add to God—*nothing*! There is nothing that we can add to the blood of Jesus—*nothing*! There is nothing that we can add to the Holy Spirit—*nothing*! Yet the devil is trying to get you to drag your prayer life, your Word life, and your worship into the equation of God's power being manifest. *Watch…*

The devil will speak these things to you:

* *If you spend enough quality time in prayer, God can use you.* In that mindset, the devil has lured you into bringing the quality of your prayer into the equation of God's ability to move in power.
* *If you spend more time in the Word and in commentaries and at conferences, you enhance God's ability to use you.*
* *If you spend more time praying in the Holy Ghost, you will enhance God's ability to use you more.*

Do I have your attention yet?

The devil has lured myriads of believers into *doing more* and seeing less of God's power. Why is this? God is God all by Himself.

If we believe that we have to interject ourselves into the equation of God's power to see Him move, we have tainted the equation.

There are multitudes of believers trying to read more, pray more, hear more, straining to make themselves more usable and not realizing that in doing all of this, they are trying to make themselves more usable *by their own hands.*

The resulting frustration has led *good* people right out the door of the church. We do *not* make ourselves more usable by what we do; we have to trust in the power of the name of Jesus *only*!

So in my own struggles, the Holy Spirit asked me this question, "What about *the Jesus you forgot*? You know, the One who would move in *power* through you *when you were a heathen*. Why would He do that? Simply because it was in a time when your total dependency was on the power of His name and *not* your actions, however religious they were!"

> *"If we believe that we have to interject ourselves into the equation of God's power to see Him move, we have tainted the equation."*

Now as the lame man who was healed held on to Peter and John, all the people ran together to them in the porch which is called Solomon's, greatly amazed. So when Peter saw it, he responded to the people: "Men of Israel, why do you marvel at this? Or why look so intently at us, as though by our own power or godliness we had made this man walk? The God of Abraham, Isaac, and Jacob, the God of our fathers, glorified His Servant Jesus, whom you delivered up and denied in the presence of Pilate, when he was determined to let Him go. But you denied the Holy One and the Just, and asked for a murderer to be granted to you, and killed the Prince of life, whom God raised from

the dead, of which we are witnesses. And
His name, *through faith in His name,* has
made this man strong, whom you see
and know. Yes, the faith which comes
through Him has given him this perfect
soundness in the presence of you all.
(Acts 3:11–16 NKJV)

Peter had already gone through that part of his life,
where he was trying to be strong enough, trying to be right
enough, trying to say the right things passionately enough to
be used of God. *But* in Acts 3, we find that Peter realized that
it was all about *faith in the power of the name of Jesus!*

My own salvation experience taught me something:
While I could never do enough to satisfy my dad, my Father
in heaven had already loved me enough to rescue me *before*
I could bring any value to Him. The *power of God* is in the
name of *Jesus,* not our works! It is in who He is, not what
we do! We bring nothing to the table except our *trust* in the
power of His name.

Chapter 7

Why Today's Church Is Struggling

*R*eligion will lead more people into sin than the sin itself.

Being that I was raised in the South, one of the things that really stands out in my upbringing was the fact that we were really outdoorsmen. I spent a great deal of time in the woods growing up. My senior year of high school, I trapped, skinned, stretched out, and sold 110 raccoon hides in the month of November 1978. I did this by running traps before daylight, 'coon hunting several nights a week, and all while I was working a part-time job and going to high school.

I actually saw a raccoon once that someone had caught in a live trap and nursed him back to health at home in a cage. That raccoon would move from one side of the cage to the other constantly, with his face and hands pressed tightly to the bottom edge of the cage. He was going back and forth, looking at the exact same corners for hours on end as though the next time he looked, he might see an opening to escape. It seemed like pure insanity, which it is.

I believe that religion is the exact same way and the greatest weapon used by Satan to trap people into ineffectiveness in their walk with God. Religion will lead more people into sin than the sin itself.

The reason is simple: Religion forces your decisions and actions to be centered on what you do instead of what Jesus has already done. Religion leads a person to think about how their actions should open the door to God's moving, therefore taking the focus off God's power and putting it on their actions.

Should we pray? *Absolutely*! Should we read the word of God? *Absolutely*! Should we fellowship with other believers? *Absolutely*! Should we pray in the Spirit? *Absolutely*! But all of these should usher us into an even *deeper* trust in the power of His name instead of trusting in what we are doing.

The church has been led into a mindset of "if you are struggling, you just need to *do* x, y, z more," which only has the power to lead you into thinking that everything will turn to the good by *your own actions*. The reality is that this mindset can and will eventually lead you to focusing more on your own actions than God's power!

What about the Jesus I forgot, the one who moved in power through someone who was not even saved and did so simply because he believed in the power of the name of Jesus! What about this power that is available to all who believe, not in their own actions but the power of the name of Jesus because it is available to all who believe!

I know this is controversial to so many, but so was Jesus, and that is the entire point. Every action that we take moving us toward Jesus—our prayer life, our Word life, our fellowship with other believers, our worship, our praying in the Holy Spirit—should cause us to trust the power of His name more, not ourselves.

The devil is always lurking in the shadows, trying to pervert, even if it is just ever so subtly, that which is holy and pure. When you pray and you see the answer, the devil says, "It was because you prayed. It was because of how you prayed. It was because you sought the Lord. It was because of your knowledge in the Word. It was because of you. It was because of you. *It was because of you!*"

Everything good that happens through you is not because of you. It can only be because you believe in the power of the name of Jesus. There is power in no other, regardless of who they are.

> Do not be deceived, my beloved brethren. Every good gift and every perfect gift is from above, and comes down from the Father of lights, with whom there is no variation or shadow of turning. Of His own will He brought us forth by the word of truth, that we might be a kind of firstfruits of His creatures. (James 1:16–18 NKJV)

If we do not recognize the enemy's plot against the body of Christ, we will grow more and more confident in ourselves and God using us because of who we think we are, to the point that God Himself will refrain from answering our prayers. He will not do this to hurt us but to liberate us from chasing after a self-righteous religion.

When we are basing all the good things happening in our lives on our own righteousness, God knows that by hindering us from obtaining what we want, even in the good things, this will lead us to frustration and maybe a deep enough frustration to seek Him out.

When this reality is hidden from us because of the subtle lies of darkness, we get caught in a rut. It looks just like that raccoon going back and forth, doing the same things over and over again, hoping for a different result. The more we are not seeing God move, the more we try to do the things we know we need to do, but we are doing them because we believe that our doing will get Him to move. The resulting frustration will begin to open the door to looking for other things that might make us feel a little more satisfied with ourselves. This will eventually lead to sin and walking away from God.

Self is at the center of all sin, and it is why Satan will use religion to lead people away from God by getting them to focus more on what they are doing than who Jesus is! God's word does not lead us into the mindset of God performing our will but just the opposite. We are called out of selfishness to conform our will to His.

There will always be that portion of folks who will say, "What about where the Scriptures says, 'Whatsoever you shall ask…'"? That is taken completely out of context by the kingdom of darkness to drag yourself right back into the center of the conversation.

Take this for example:

> Delight yourself also in the Lord, And He
> shall give you the desires of your heart.
> (Psalm 37:4 NKJV)

The religious will try to use this passage to justify their cause of getting God to do what their heart desires, but that mindset is missing what the Scripture says. For you to delight yourself in the Lord means that *His will* becomes your delight; His purposes become your plan; His passions become your motivation. When this happens, it is because *who God is* has transformed your heart. Getting to the point of God giving you the desires of your heart is because your heart lines up with His!

The crux of the matter is that people struggle with the lordship of Jesus. Most people come to Jesus because they want to escape hell. In other words, they have heard a message that *only* the blood of Jesus covers our sins, and they want that debt paid for, but there is a problem.

> But grow in the grace and knowledge
> of our Lord and Savior Jesus Christ. To
> Him be the glory both now and forever.
> Amen. (2 Peter 3:18 NKJV)

There are so many references in the word of God that refer to Jesus as *Lord and Savior*, therefore He is *both* Lord and Savior. You cannot separate Jesus from who He is. In other words, you cannot make Jesus your Savior and reject Him as Lord. Either Jesus is both Lord and Savior or He is neither.

The entire strategy of Satan is to lure people into making their relationship with Jesus as Savior only. Knowing this will create a dynamic where *we* are at the center, and Jesus is there to do our bidding. There is no one that would make that statement out loud, but people's frustrations with God reveal it, and this reality always ends up with sin dominating the scene.

I have a question to ask: Is Jesus Christ the Lord of your life? I want you to notice that I did not ask if Jesus was your Savior but if He was your Lord. If Jesus is Lord, then everything about Him and His word must be true: His plans for you are for good only and not for harm; He is Alpha and Omega; He formed you in the womb before the foundation of this world; He has called you by name… If all of this is true, then we should trust Him.

If we say that we trust Him, then anything He asks and any direction He gives, our only response must be, "Yes, *Lord!*"

If we struggle with His word or His leading, then it can only be because of one solitary reason: We do not trust Him as Lord.

Everything is wrapped up in the lordship of Jesus. If you are wrestling with what the spirit of Jesus is leading you to do, this can only mean that you are still lord of your own life. You have yet to make Jesus *Lord!* You are not wrestling with faith. Faith says that Jesus is *Lord.* Everything else is willing obedience to His lordship!

When there is a wrestling with the lordship of Jesus, this is where we enter the subtitle of this book: *Have we sacrificed obedience on the altars of reason?* Have we literally reached a place in our lives where we believe that our rationale is more important than what God says? The only reason for this to take place is due to placing ourselves into God's equation, distorting every aspect of a pure relationship with God!

So how do we get back to that place where He is free to be Lord in and through our lives again? Excellent questions deserve excellent answers.

Have we sacrificed obedience on the altars of reason?

Chapter 8

Warfare for Faith

Evaluation

By now the Lord has brought up some areas of your life that you may have been dealing with, and I hope that you are still engaged in this conversation. I call it a conversation because I *know* that you have responded probably out loud to some of the statements made herein, but I also know that by you continuing to read, God is speaking to you. I believe that you are reading this little book because you are hungry for God and want to see Him moving in and through your life. So let's get started with what it takes to get back to the place where Jesus is *Lord* in our lives.

First step is to take *all* of your prayer request and do the absolute *warfare* necessary to push them aside. That is correct; your first step in entering back into the arena of faith, where God moves in the miraculous, is to do the warfare necessary to give Him *first place* in your life again.

We do not read the word of God to get Him to answer our prayer. We do *not* worship God to get Him to answer our prayer. We do *not* get involved in ministry to get God to answer our prayer.

It is as though our prayer request have become more important to us than God Himself, and I will prove it. *What has consumed most of your time with God lately?*

The enemy wants you to spend all your time with God focused on what you want or need or even what someone else needs, just so that God will not be your focus. So I am challenging you to evaluate your prayer life to see if God is the focus of your time with Him, *or* are your prayer requests the central theme of all your time with Him?

One morning, I was in prayer and praying over a particular counseling situation, and the Holy Spirit spoke to me concerning that need. I immediately said "thank You, Lord!" to the person of the Holy Spirit. That is correct; we need to develop a relationship with the person of the Holy Spirit because we do not even know how to pray as we ought.

But when I said "thank You, Lord!" He immediately spoke back and said, "Are you going to stop there?" Suddenly, I realized that he was implying that I could make my entire time with Him about *only* what I wanted from Him.

Stunned and excited about His leading, I literally reached my hand in front of me, as if I were grabbing what He had spoken to me concerning that need, and moved it behind my back and said, "No, sir, I want You!" As I continued in prayer, He began to reveal things about another counseling situation, and once again I said, "Thank You, Lord!" And once again, He said, "Are you going to stop there?"

This continued with Him speaking to me about my finances, my children, and even my marriage. But with each passing revelation, I grabbed those revelations and put them behind me as though they might be blocking me from getting to Him.

Then His *glory* fell all around me, and I was completely overwhelmed. He told me, "Because you have warred your way through what you wanted from Me, to get to Me, I want you to turn around and speak over each of those areas in which I spoke to you *from my presence*. Because when My word goes forth from My presence, it never returns to Me void!"

I instantly began to *war* over each of those areas that the Lord revealed to me. One example was while I was speaking from God's presence over a lady I was counseling, these are the words that the Spirit led me to pray: "You foul seed of discord, that has set itself up against my sister's heart concerning spiritual authority, *I bind you in Jesus's name!*"

Later that day when I called her, she immediately cut me off and said, "Pastor Lane, before you say anything else, I need to repent to you for harboring seeds of discord against God's spiritual authority."

I almost dropped the phone. The very words that were spoken from God's presence by His leading were spoken back to me almost verbatim.

That evening, as I was pondering these events before the Lord, I asked Him what had taken place that day, and this is what the Holy Spirit revealed to me: Imagine a dart board with the bull's-eye being God's presence. Then imagine all the rings around the bull's-eye being our prayer request, with the outside rings being the least important to the innermost ring being the most important. Now imagine people starting on the outside with their prayer request then getting the answers they are looking for and *then leaving*.

They may not leave at the outermost request, but when they get the answers to what they are most looking for, they turn around and leave. Why? Because they were *not* seeking God's presence. They did *not* want to hear His heart and His passions. All they wanted was the answers to what they wanted.

Then the Lord said to me, "When you are willing to do the warfare it takes to push anything and everything else to the side, including your own prayer request, in order to get to My presence, you will find yourself in My presence. That is the place where I reveal who I am, and I can lead you into praying *My will* over everything you have in your heart. But most are *not* willing to do that kind of warfare!"

Faith

Faith is not something that you have to muster up. You either *know* that you know, or you are going to *fake it until you make it*, which is cliché for religion in the heavenly realms. When I made it into God's presence, I didn't pray *by faith*, like most religious folks say, which is another way of saying that they do *not* believe it but are going to pray for it anyway.

In that moment of being in the presence of the living God, I was no longer praying from my ignorance, from my religiosity, from my hopes and desires—*no*, I was praying from an absolute assurance because I wasn't leading the prayer, I was following the leading of the Holy Spirit.

The enemy of our souls has led many people into believing that hope and faith are the same, and they are *not*. Hoping for something means that we are believing that it might happen one day. Faith means that God, through His Word and His spirit, has declared something to be finished, and we *know* that it can't *not* happen. Please excuse the double negatives!

The body of Christ has to war against anything and everything that would cause our faith to be polluted. When we pray according to the Bible's definition of faith, the only reason we would *not* receive what we are believing for is because God has a bigger plan than what we are asking of Him.

Jesus asked three times for His Father to not make Him drink of the cup of suffering that was coming, and the Father said *no* to His Son!

But it was only because the Father had a greater plan than to please His Son; it was our salvation; it was our deliverance; it was our freedom; and it was to draw us to Himself so that He could manifest what true faith is in the earth.

What possible reason could there be to *not* do the warfare for this kind of faith? This is not super faith; it is simply faith.

All of this book is leading in one direction: Faith in the power of the name of Jesus becomes a lifestyle when we get ourselves out of the way and allow Jesus to be *Lord* of our lives again. When this happens, there is something transformative that takes place in our lives.

Chapter 9

The Peace of God

So Gideon built an altar there to the Lord,
and called it The-Lord-Is-Peace.

—Judges 6:24 NKJV

Jehovah Shalom

When Gideon was speaking to the *Angel of the Lord*, who is a reference of Jesus in the Old Testament and the reason some versions of the Bible capitalize the letter A when referring to the angel of the Lord, when Gideon saw that it was actually the Lord, he thought he was going to die because he had seen God's face.

I believe that there are tons of believers out there who are afraid of going into the presence of God today because they are afraid that God will ask more of them than they are willing to give. In other words, they believe that they would basically die.

But when the Angel of the Lord said in verse 23, "Peace be with you; do not fear, you shall not die," in that moment, Gideon called Him *Jehovah Shalom, the Lord is peace.* He didn't wait to see if what He had said would come to pass; he believed that He was the Lord and that He was peace.

From that moment on, Gideon went forward with *everything* the Lord directed him to do—in *peace*! He was no longer afraid because the Lord Himself was with him. How can you fail if the Lord is leading you where He desires? We can only fail if we are the ones leading ourselves or we are being led by someone else.

But the Lord always leads us besides still waters. He leads us into green pastures, and it is *He* who restores our souls. He even makes a banquet table filled with the best feast to eat to our full, right in front of all of our enemies. *Peace*!

When we realize that Jesus is *Lord* of lords, and there is *none* besides Him, and push everything else to the side because we *trust* in the power of His name, then please tell me what weapon formed against you can prosper?

Then, we have peace, not within ourselves but in Him to go forward with whatever it is that He asks without fear and trembling. Follow the peace of God, not the peace of rationalization. I need to ask this question again, "Have we sacrificed obedience on the altars of reason?"

The only reason to sidestep obedience is because we are wrestling with His lordship.

But when He is *Lord*, and this is established in our hearts, whatever He requests of us becomes our highest honor to apply.

Even if He leads you into something that you have no training, if it is King Jesus who is leading you, He knows what He wants to do in the process. Just look at the early apostles when they stood before the religious leaders of that day and were following the Holy Spirit's lead. The religious leaders had to take note that while these men were uneducated, they could not refute the wisdom that came from them.

Saints, I am not saying that getting educated is bad, but what I am saying is that when you totally depend on your education and not the Lord, you have put yourself into the equation of God moving through your life. Just remember this, what about *The Jesus I forgot*—the One who moved in *power* through someone who had nothing to use—except faith, and that was enough! Make every decision in your life based on this *peace*, that the Prince of peace is more than enough to lead you and guide you.

When my daughters were considering getting married, I brought those young men before my Father and asked if they were going to be my sons-in-law, and the peace of God came all over me.

In one case, though I had set aside one hour to pray over this young man, the Lord moved so quickly with His answer that I looked at my watch and said, "I have fifty-nine and a half minutes to pray about something else!"

So my youngest daughter, Rebecca, started the courtship process with this young man, and about two to three months in, they broke it off. My wife came to me and said, "I thought you heard from God concerning who she should marry."

I said to her, "He has never lied to me!"

A couple months later, God had moved on their hearts, and they began the process again. The end result was that thirty-five people gave their hearts to Jesus at their wedding!

> For we walk by faith, not by sight.
> (2 Corinthians 5:7 NKJV)

Walking in faith instead of what you are seeing, feeling, and fretting is called *peace*. You do *not* get this kind of peace from the world's ways. It isn't rationalizing things by weighing out the options. It is solely because you have come to the point where there is only one option: Wherever the Prince of peace leads, that is my answer!

It is my prayer that you will have taken what you have read on these few pages, allowed this revelation to reveal something about your own walk with God and turn you toward Him in such a way as to never look back. Chase after, and place your trust in His peace, and you will have peace like Gideon, even the peace to go to war with the kingdom of darkness, knowing that *greater is He that is in you than he that is in the world.*

Conclusion

The Greatest Miracle— Salvation

The greatest miracle is salvation, and this has become so convoluted throughout history that many, even in the church world, have totally lost their purity. If you are reading this little book because the Lord caught your attention with the title or someone passed it on to you, just realize that this Jesus *loves you*.

I know that all the mistakes you have made in your life and the terrible things that life has thrown at you may have caused you to question His love for you, but I want to prove to you that He does in fact love you.

> But God demonstrates His own love toward us, in that while we were still sinners, Christ died for us. (Romans 5:8 NKJV)

God isn't waiting for you to be good enough to rescue; He so loved you that before you could do anything worthy of His love, He sent His Son, Jesus, to pay the punishment price for your sins. He knew that you would *never* be able to pay for your own sins because God made such a high price for the payment of sin: pure, innocent, holy blood.

Since all mankind has sinned, no one could pay that price except for Jesus! Everyone has seen this passage:

> For God so loved the world that He gave His only begotten Son, that whoever believes in Him should not perish but have everlasting life. (John 3:16 NKJV)

But they feel that they have either done too much wrong to be deserving of this kind of love, *or* they tried to live right and have messed up time and again, creating a sense of unworthiness of His love. If either of these fits you, read the very next passage, and you will find out that God is madly in love with you and for you.

> For God did not send His Son into the world to condemn the world, but that the world through Him might be saved. (John 3:17 NKJV)

If you have never given your heart to Jesus before, *or* you have at some point in your life but you walked away for any reason, His mighty hand of loving kindness is reaching out to you *right now*! If you are willing to accept His love and not only have your sins forgiven (mercy) but also walk in the power of being a child of God (grace), simply pray this prayer out loud:

> Father, I know that I am a sinner, and I do not deserve your Love for me. I also know that I cannot pay for my sin but you Loved me so much that You sent Your Son Jesus and He took my punishment, He paid my price for sin. Forgive me Lord as I repent of my sin. Cover my sin with the blood of Jesus. Fill me with Your Holy Spirit, and from this day forward, Jesus is *Lord* of my life!

If you prayed that prayer in *faith* and meant it, the greatest miracle just took place; you are born again. Your decision is the very cause of all of heaven rejoicing.

> I say to you that likewise there will be more joy in heaven over one sinner who repents than over ninety-nine just persons who need no repentance. (Luke 15:7 NKJV)

This is not the end of the matter, only the beginning. Get plugged into a church that teaches the word of God, and begin to live out this great salvation.

Be ignited

If you are already born again, this revelation of *all* power being in the name of Jesus alone and not in our works or deeds should cause you to start feeling a little bit of release about now. Not only are you feeling a release from trying to do enough to be used by God, but you are feeling ignited to start walking in the *power* of the name of Jesus, as a child of God should.

The mercy of God is what ushers you into forgiveness, but it is the grace of God that gives you sonship.

> But if the Spirit of Him who raised Jesus from the dead dwells in you, He who raised Christ from the dead will also give life to your mortal bodies through His Spirit who dwells in you. (Romans 8:11 NKJV)

Walk in, and release that same power through your faith. Your faith is in His name, which is the power to save you, and it alone is what has the power to save others through you. It is not you but your faith in the power of the name of *Jesus*; that is the gospel.

This is why the apostles of New Testament Church were able to do such great acts of faith because it was acts of faith In the name of Jesus! If you receive and apply this word, you will be ignited with a passion for God, and you will begin to see the glory of God in your life again!

I would like to offer my deepest appreciation to my family and our wonderful church family at New Life Church of Abbeville, La for the incredible love and support throughout the years.

—Pastor Lane Payne

If this revelation has spoken to you, we would love to hear your feedback. Please contact us at thejesusiforgot.com.

About the Author

L ane was brought up in the small town of Baker, Louisiana. The son of a hardworking plumber, who was a completely no-nonsense kind of man. Lane was exposed to the things of God growing up but did not get saved until thirty years of age, and that is when everything in his life was transformed. That transformation led him to leave a position at Exxon Chemical Plant in Baton Rouge, Louisiana, to becoming a pastor at Bethany World Prayer Center, to starting a church in Abbeville, Louisiana, merging that church with another and forming New Life Church. He pastored that church for twenty years before running for United States congress and eventually writing *The Jesus I Forgot*. After retiring as pastor of New Life Church, he created a new ministry, Genos Ministries, to bring an evangelistic anointing back to the local church. This book was written as a documentary about his journey, and he is sharing it to reach those who have struggled in their walk with or their concept of God.

.

Printed in the USA
CPSIA information can be obtained
at www.ICGtesting.com
LVHW052333011024
792701LV00002B/234